PROSE AND KAHNS

ZACK KAHN

© 2011

http://www.proseandkahns.com

Published in the United States by Paradisiac Publishing Inc.

http://www.theparadisiacgroup.com

ISBN: 978-0985316884

Back cover photo by Powell Weaver.

THIS BOOK IS DEDICATED TO
ALL THE TEACHERS WHO TOLD ME
I'D NEVER AMOUNT TO NOTHIN'.

DON'T YOU
HATE IT
WHEN YOU
THINK YOU
REALLY KNOW
SOMEONE AND
IT TURNS
OUT TO JUST
BE 2 LITTLE
KIDS IN A GIANT
OVERCOAT?

I'VE MET DONALD DUCK LIKE 4 TIMES NOW BUT HE NEVER REMEMBERS ME!

UNCLE SAM
WAS ACTUALLY
POINTING TO
THE TALL
DUDE BEHIND YOU.

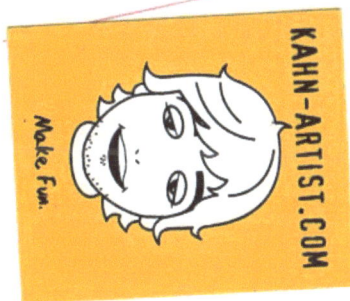

I KNOW YOU
SHOULD NEVER
SHIT WHERE
YOU EAT, BUT
I HAD TO
MAKE AN
EXCEPTION
AT P.F.
CHANG'S =

It's hard to find
Friends with benefits
in this economy.

F7

10

You can tell ~~(scribbled out)~~
a movie
character is evil
if they're poorly-lit,
smoking cigarettes,
or Steve Buscemi.

INVENTION IDEA!!

CORDLESS
GARDEN
HOSE
(LOGISTICS
TBD)

(→ Buy CordlessGardenHose.com)

ENDORSE HERE

_____

_____

_____

_____

DO NOT WRITE, STAMP OR SIGN BELOW THIS LINE
RESERVED FOR FINANCIAL INSTITUTION USE *

do you think Abraham Lincoln was assassinated for political reasons or 'cuz his hat was in the way?

I GOT 99 PROBLEMS AND MATH IS 2 OF THEM.

BURGER

Today, I went swimming

or, as fish say, "went."

IF YOU FOLD THE EDGES
OF A DOLLAR BILL
JUST RIGHT, YOU
LOOK LIKE A FUCKING
IDIOT.

My friend
works as a mascot
for Merriam-Webster.
He's like a walking dictionary.

I saw a black cop and a white cop together today but nothing funny happened!

I HAD
A GARAGE
SALE
BUT NOBODY
BOUGHT IT.

i'm gonna start getting the paper delivered just so I have someone to play catch with.

how the fuck are we gonna find our way out of this breadcrumb factory?

BUT ENOUGH ABOUT PEE, LET'S TALK ABOUT POO!

I like my
women like
I like my
coffee.

Hilarious.

Kahn

SOMETIMES
DREAMS REALLY
DO COME TRUE!

TODAY, I WAS CHASED
BY A GIANT TACO

"AIRBORNE" WAS CREATED BY AN ELEMENTARY SCHOOL TEACHER BUT I THINK IT WOULD BE WAY MORE EFFECTIVE IF IT WAS CREATED BY A CHEMIST.

For "Emergency Contact,"
I always write "911"
'cuz ~~scribble~~
Cousin
Greg doesn't
know shit.

Be Mine

-Zack

They say the ghost of Elvis
haunts the Roosevelt Hotel.

I guess that's the one building
he hasn't left.

Fluorescent light bulbs lack confidence.

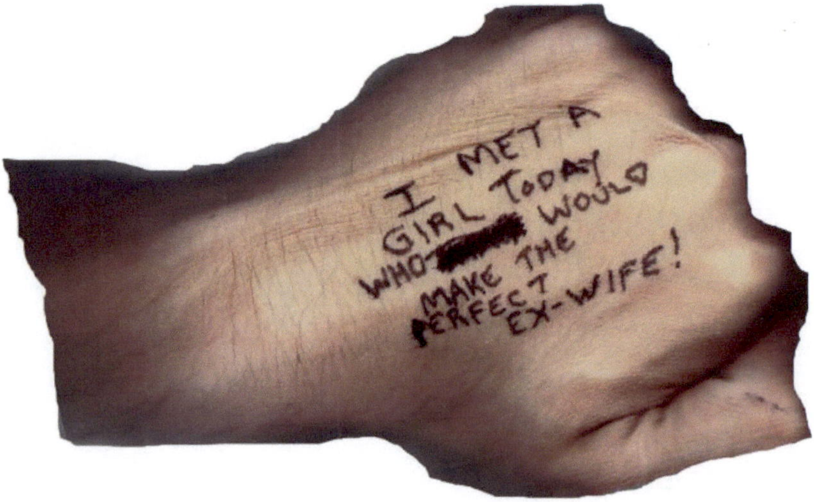

what you should know about

SEXUAL
HARASSMENT

a guide for
administrators, faculty, staff and students

They say
the camera
adds 10 lbs.
So I stopped
carrying a
camera.

You can't hurry love.
Especially if you've
been drinking whiskey

DISSECTING FROGS
IN SCHOOL TEACHES
YOU IMPORTANT
LIFE LESSONS
LIKE HOW TO TAKE
APART A FROG

WELCOME TO WA...

TO MAKE A LONG STORY SHORT, JUST SHUT THE FUCK UP

MANAGED BY

PAY CASHIER ON WAY OUT

PARK & LOCK

209-553

I finally
proposed to her
but she hasn't
texted me back yet.

I forgot that I stashed
ecstasy in my Mucinex bottle.

I'm still congested but it feels
fucking AMAZING!!!

I KNOW A
GIRL WHO
PRACTICES MODERN-
DAY WITCHCRAFT.
SHE FLIES
AROUND ON
A SWIFFER.

I have so much
emotional
baggage that I
have to pay an
extra fee when
I travel.

if you have ~~[image]~~

nothing nice to

Say, maybe

TMZ is

hiring!

I Was Writing This
Awesome Haiku When
I Totally Got Distracted By
A Text Message

SO MANY
GREAT
ETCH-A-SKETCH
ARTISTS
FADE
AWAY BEFORE
THEIR TIME.

PEOPLE
WHO
LiVE
iN
GLASS
Houses
SHOULD
GeT
STONED

I LOVE MY
ADOPTED
HIGHWAY

AS IF IT
WE'RE MY
OWN CEMENT.

IF DOGS
COULD
talk, I
bet they'd
all sound
like Johnny
Cash.

Man, it used to
be about rock,
 paper, scissors
with you. Now,
it's just all
      scissors!

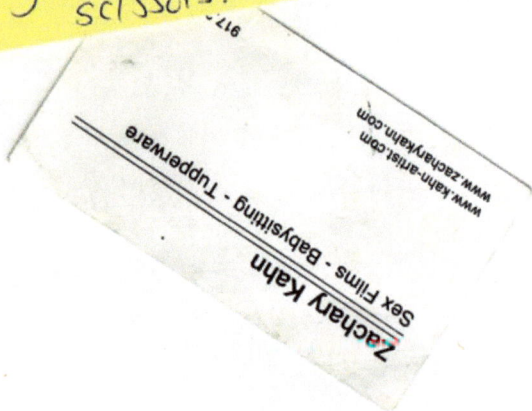

Zachary Kahn
Sex Films - Babysitting - Tupperware

www.kahn-artist.com
www.zacharykahn.com
917...

I AIN'T SAYING SHE'S A GOLD DIGGER, BUT SHE DOES OWN A METAL DETECTOR!

THEY SAY "YOU ARE WHAT YOU EAT," SO I APOLOGIZE IF I'M TOTALLY COMING OFF LIKE A TUNA SANDWICH ON VALIUM

domains to renew ⚡↑!!
↓ !!!

- AMERICAS NEXT TOP WHATEVER .com
- itriedthatincollege.com
- UNDERTHEBARACK.com
- letsgosmokeajoint.com
- SODRUNKRIGHTNOW.com
- HOTCHICKSWITHASTHMA.com
- YouDontKnowHowItFeels.com
- IWILLFUCKINGCUT YOU.com
- Meetmeinthebathroom.com
- ilovebobmarley.com
- Stonercomedy.com
- stonerhumor.com
- obamainpajamas.com

I GUESS THE one THing Meat Loaf won't do for love is exercise.

I THREW A
COIN INTO A
FOUNTAIN ON
HOLLYWOOD BLVD.
BUT IT SPIT IT
BACK OUT
BECAUSE IT WASN'T
TAKING UNSOLICITED
SUBMISSIONS AT
THIS TIME.

a note from:
Zachary Kahn

I'LL NEVER REMEMBER WHERE
I WAS THE DAY I FOUND OUT
I HAD AMNESIA

I CAN'T
AFFORD
THERAPY
SO I JUST
EAT A LOT
OF FORTUNE
COOKIES

I'LL NEVER REMEMBER WHERE I WAS THE DAY I FOUND OUT I HAD AMNESIA

With
Books-on-
Tape, you can
ATTACH BOOKS TO
ANYTHING!

I'm not a
sex offender
but I do like
to meet the
neighbors!

I think it's
time we let
Slinkies use the
elevator.

the early bird
may
get the worm
but he always misses
out on the Tequila

I'm dating
a Rubik's Cube.

It's complicated.

I've been flying a kite all year but I still haven't discovered shit!

Hammocks are for sleepy people who like danger.

12   Oct. 3   (   ) 1

    ORDER   rder #1

QTY ITEM
1 RE DER DONE
1 O CK S TO-OR.   3 7
1 DO BLE   BURGER   2

S   6 9
Tax   0.61
Take-Out To al

Cashless
Change   0 0

MER   07/0
CARD ISU   ACCOUNT
Maste   20   ###8475
AUT ORIZ   SE H 25370.

MCDONAL

I WANNA BE A SCREENWRITER. WHAT'S THE BEST COFFEE SHOP FOR THAT?

IF SOMETHING
IS NOT BUTTER,
PLEASE JUST
FUCKiNG TELL ME!

I HATE
SURPRISES

A MAGICIAN FOUND A
QUARTER IN MY EAR
SO I SCHEDULED AN MRI
FOR THURSDAY.

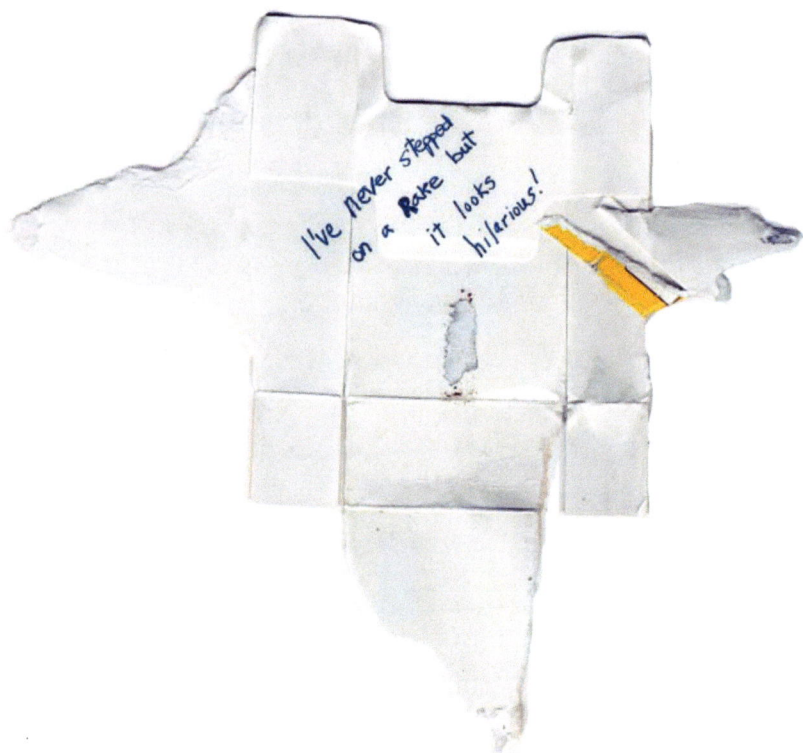

I've never stepped on a Rake but it looks hilarious!

IN COLLEGE,
MY THESIS
PAPER HAD TO BE
50,000 WORDS SO
I JUST SUBMITTED
50 PICTURES.

I wanna get a
scratch-off
tattoo so when
it goes out of style,
I might win
something!

KAHN-
Make fun.

One of
my buddies
is a mime
but he never
talks about it.

1176

WELL, SPACE CAMP'S BE FUCKIN' PROVED TO BE FUCKIN' COMPLETE WASTE.

PINATAS WERE MADE TO BE BROKEN

POSTCARDS ARE COOL
UNLESS YOU'RE TALKING
SHIT ABOUT

THE MAILMAN.

I'M USUALLY INTO
S+M BUT I'LL TAKE A LARGE
IF THAT'S ALL
THEY HAVE

I WAS DRIVING THROUGH MIDDLE AMERICA WHEN I CAME TO A SPORK IN THE ROAD

I spilled bong water on
my magic carpet and now
it keeps pulling over for snacks.

I USED TO
BE REALLY
INTO FANTASY
FOOTBALL UNTIL
I TORE MY
FANTASY
ROTATOR
CUFF

Life will open doors
for you if you
have a good heart and
respect others.

or if you're hot.

IF YOU'RE EVER LOST IN THE DARK, JUST GET AN IDEA!

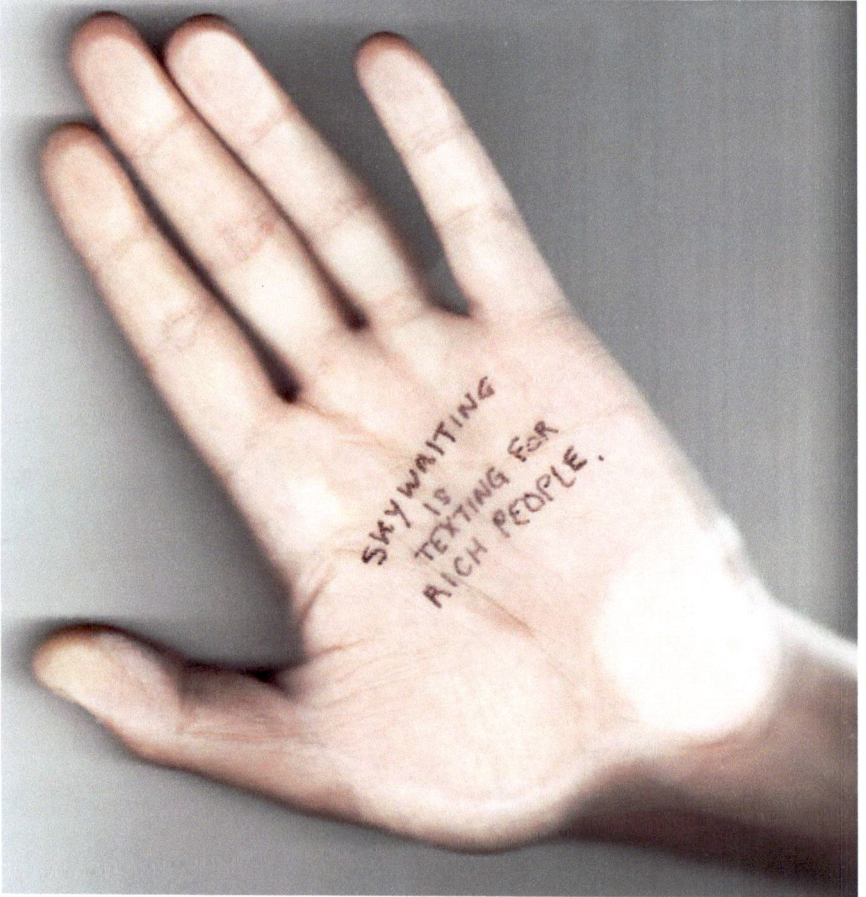

Are there any
  Subway Sandwich Artists
left who aren't just
      in it for the
Money?

$

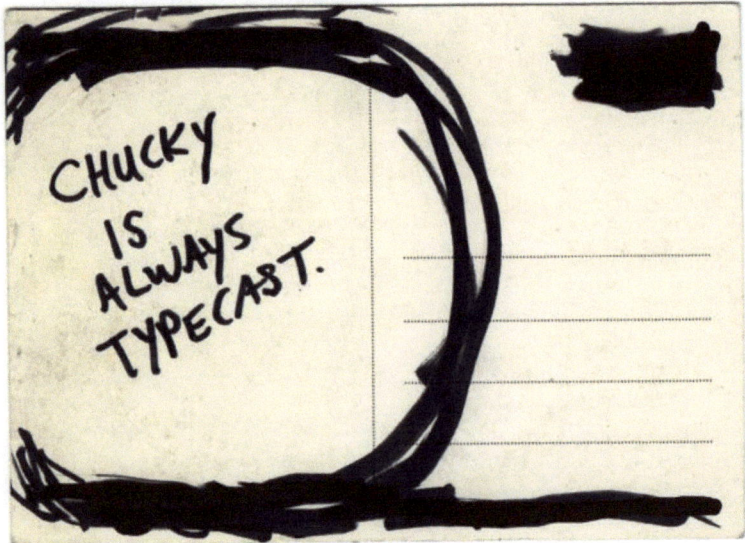

CHUCKY
IS
ALWAYS
TYPECAST.

People online are so
mean to each other.

Tweet others as
you wish to
be tweeted!

I just
walked past
Barnes + Noble
and from the looks of
those covers, they
got some nice
books in there!

IF MORE
PEOPLE
FOLLOWED
THEIR DREAMS,
THERE'D BE NO
NEED FOR
ROCK N'ROLL
FANTASY
CAMPS.

SPECIAL THANKS

You.

For Booking Information

(310) 279-0855

booking@paradisiacpublishing.com

www.ingramcontent.com/pod-product-compliance
Lightning Source LLC
Chambersburg PA
CBHW042128080426
42735CB00001B/10